Bird —
memories of
walks here
Jennie
10-17

ON FISHER POND

*Memories of Bill Fisher and
His Gift to Vashon Island*

ON FISHER POND

Memories of Bill Fisher and
His Gift to Vashon Island

LAURIE BEVAN STEWART

ENDICOTT AND HUGH BOOKS

We greatly appreciate the photographers who generously contributed their work to this book: Jeff Dunnicliff, Jen Joynt, Marvin Kellar, Martin Koenig, and Peter Murray; and our staff field trips to Fisher Pond with Julian White-Davis.

To be in intimate contact with the land like this is to enclose it in the same moral universe we occupy, to include it in the meaning of the word community.

~ BARRY LOPEZ

I PASS BY FISHER Pond every day on my way to town. Often I stop and walk through the orchard of apples and plums past the green metal barn where Bill used to live. I cross the grassy yard once filled with his clutter of trucks and machinery. I enter the cool and damp of the woods, and walk the familiar path to where I look out over the length of the pond. I sit by a granite boulder engraved with these words:

FISHER POND
STEWARDED WITH VISION
BY BILL FISHER SINCE 1966
DONATED TO THE LAND TRUST
FOR PERMANENT PROTECTION
1998

1

I used to sit here with Bill, watching the birds and talking. He liked the pond best in early morning when sunrise turned the clouds to flame – fire in the sky, he called it. I didn't know him well, just as a neighbor, really, but I had many fond memories of my times with him, as did many others who were lucky enough to know him.

Just after Bill's memorial service in 2002, I spoke with a number of islanders who told me stories about him, and I learned more about the history of his remarkable stewardship of the pond. As 2018 will mark the 20th anniversary of Bill's generous donation, it seemed a good time to share these stories, to remember a quiet man who gave his hard-won property in return for the promise it would be preserved for wildlife. He lived a simple, frugal life here in his later years, devoting his resources to the land. Now, protected by the Vashon-Maury Island Land Trust, Fisher Pond remains an island refuge for all the living things Bill Fisher loved and cared for.

FISHER POND IS Vashon Island's largest body of water, headwaters to Shinglemill Creek where ravens nest and wild salmon still come to spawn. In years of good rain, water spills from the east end into the tumbledown course of the Shinglemill, flowing north to Fern Cove and out to Colvos Passage and Puget Sound. But before that, water finds its way here, through seeps and trickles, runnels and rivulets, into the hollow of the pond. For a time it becomes a part of this place, gathered and held, its motion stilled. It comes here, as I do, to rest.

Fisher Pond hasn't always been a quiet refuge. It was more of a boggy field at first and there are reports of peat being dug from the east end. Bill told one interviewer that during WWI it was drained so the acreage could be commercially farmed, as part grazing pasture and part vegetable garden. Produce was transported by Splinter Fleet boats into Pike Place Market for sale. Glass greenhouses were later built on the property that eventually collapsed under heavy snow, and shards of that glass still turn up occasionally today. At least one parcel was completely logged. Another supported a mink farm into the 1960s.

It was around that time Bill Fisher started looking for land on Vashon. He had previously bought properties on the west coast of Vancouver Island and in the San Juans, but found them "a bit too dangerous" and daunting to get to. "I wasn't very rugged," he said, "but I still wanted a place. I liked the outdoors." A telephone company worker who never married, Bill started coming to Vashon from West Seattle to visit his sister. "I liked it real well, and I didn't have to drive too far to get here. I was out with a real estate dealer one day, and I saw the pond and discovered there was 60 acres with it, and that fit my budget pretty well at the time. So I bought that."

Several landowners, including the mink farmers, held other parcels of land adjacent to the pond. Over the years, Bill kept watching, buying

each one as it came up for sale, five parcels in all. "I bought the last piece in 1976 and that completed the scenery around the pond. The total is about 90 acres."

For years Bill lived in a tiny trailer on the property while he built his barn with its modest upstairs apartment. Meanwhile, he embarked on what would become his favorite pastime: "fooling around with the pond."

"It was referred to as Bank Road Pond when I bought it," Bill said in a recorded interview. "On some maps it's called Frenchman's Pond. And there was a woman who drew a map and called it Spirit Lake because

she saw some foggy wisps on it once that looked sort of ghostly. Then, because I bought it, a few people started to refer to it as Fisher Pond."

"The water was pretty low when I first saw it," Bill recalled. "The drainage ditch had started to fill in a little, but it was still going almost dry in the bad years. I put a dam in the ditch and then the pond did better. Later, I filled in across the east end, and put in a culvert, and that raised the level to about five feet of water, if we get enough rain. It just depends on the weather. But when it does get up to overflowing, it pretty near hits Bank Road. They won't raise the road, so I can't go any higher!" he said with a laugh.

Bill clearly had an affinity for water. I asked him once to tell me about his water-witching. He had mentioned it years earlier when I met him at a neighbor's potluck. He told me about the history of our new place, about the network of cisterns we couldn't figure out, and how he found deep water when the shallow well went dry.

"Well, I read a book on it once, and gave it a try," he said. He rummaged through a drawer and pulled out an L-shaped rod the diameter of coat-hanger wire. "You hold two of them lightly like that, by the short ends and parallel to each other, pointing straight ahead. When you walk over underground water, they cross. That's all there is to it. It doesn't work for everyone, but I seem to have the touch."

THE ONLY BUILDING remaining on the property is Bill's green metal barn. I'd visited the pond for several years but had

never been inside. One day the barn doors were wide open and we could see Bill working, so my sons and I stopped in to say hello. He was bent over the engine of his pickup truck, pouring in oil. He told the boys they could climb up onto the big tractor parked there. When he was finished – oil cap replaced, bottles disposed of, hands wiped, hood slammed shut – he asked if we'd like to come upstairs.

He showed us his family photographs, four generations framed and arranged on the wall. He pointed to an oval portrait of a blond boy – Bill at age seven with his very same grin. "Amazing, isn't it," he chuckled, "how such a cute kid can grow into such an old man?" There were books everywhere – on the table and shelves, in boxes and piles on the floor – about trees, horticulture, birds, soil, gardening, electronics, and also novels and cookbooks. Downstairs, his workshop was so crowded we could hardly move around, but it was tidy in its own way. There was a rubber fish that wiggled and sang "Take Me to the River" over and over, and when he turned it on for the boys they laughed and so did he. Cabinets, shelves, drawers and boxes held a hardware store's worth of materials, and tools on pegboard covered two of the walls. He pointed to a box of ice skates gleaned from yard sales and told the boys to take a pair each for next time the pond froze, and they did. Then he saw us to the door and said to stop by "any old time."

THAT EASY FAMILIARITY was the way he collected people. You would meet him at the pond and have a little chat, and pretty soon start seeking him out whenever you visited. Because after you knew him, a walk around the pond just wasn't the same if you didn't run into Bill.

The first people I sat down with to talk about him were two of his Bank Road neighbors, Bill Dille and Priscilla Beard. We met over tea in Priscilla's farmhouse kitchen. Bill Dille is an artist who owns acreage and a large pond across the road where he raises shaggy, long-horned cattle. "The first thing I've got to tell you is you may not find a lot of stories about Bill. He was a real private guy," Bill told me. "Sometimes we'd go out for breakfast up at The Islander. But mainly what we did for years was see each other in the woods, and we'd hang out and talk. He wasn't a scientist, but we'd pick fungus off the trees and try to analyze what was going on in the dirt. That's how I knew him mainly, in the woods, poking around or looking at birds and just sitting."

"That's kind of how I knew him, too," said Priscilla, who was the fundraising chair for the Land Trust at the time. "We usually took a walk together. I used to go down once a month and take him banana bread and check on him. Once I helped him buy a down comforter because he said he was so cold at night. But I don't have many specific stories. I mean, how do you say you took him banana bread once a month and walked around the pond? The thing about spending time with Bill was – it was hard to translate."

Even the simplest interactions with Bill could be memorable. I recall standing one day under a tree in his orchard. He was choosing apples to pick, one for each of my boys. He reached up and touched them gently, testing the stems. And he asked me, as he had before, about the trees on our farm. He knew Mike and Grace who planted nut, fruit and shade trees on our property forty years earlier. He had witched their well and still remembered how deep the water lies, how a river flows beneath our land and springs from the west side of the island. He asked me about certain plants he remembered – the corkbark oak north of the house, the loganberry along the drive, grape vines by the barn. "How's that old pear tree down front?"

"Still there," I told him, "a little scabby, but it still bears." Then he told me of a pear he once found lying beneath it, how he bent to pick it up, and bit into its flesh. "That was the sweetest pear I have ever tasted in all my life." He looked at me and smiled. And it seemed to me his eyes welled up with the memory of it – the lifting of the pear to his mouth, the warmth of its skin in his hand, and the wonder of its sweetness which had never left him.

PERHAPS THE FRIEND who knew him best was Harry Bebow. I met with Harry at the Coffee Roasterie where he often sat with a lively group of other retired gentlemen to drink coffee and talk. He spoke to me at length about his friendship with Bill.

"He was more like a brother to me than a friend. I knew him for about six years – I happened to meet him one day on the Fauntleroy ferry dock, got talking to him about his pickup truck and found out I

only lived about a mile from him. As the ferry came in I asked him if he liked going to yard sales. He said he did, so we went yard saleing the next Saturday. Then we found out his sister and my daughter both live on the Kitsap Peninsula. He was driving up there the next day and said, 'You're welcome to come along because it's a lonesome ride alone.' So we got to know each other better that way.

"He was never really lonely, though. He liked company but he liked his privacy, too. When I first got to know him he was very shy and reserved, but after about a year he seemed like a different man entirely. He had a good sense of humor. He would buy plastic alligators and turtles, and he'd put them in the pond. Then little kids would see them and yell 'Look, there's an alligator!' Oh, he'd laugh and get a kick out of that.

"There was hardly a day that I didn't see him or call him or he'd call me. He always had that grin on his face when he came out the door. He'd say, 'Whatchya selling?' Something like that. We just joked around all the time."

"I thought I was a packrat," Harry said, "but he was twice the packrat I was. He had eight trucks, six rototillers, and all sorts of stuff. He'd buy something at a yard sale and I'd say, 'What in the world do you need that for?' And he'd say, 'Well, Harry, you never know!'"

When I asked Harry about Bill's gardening, he told me the deer would discourage him. "They used to eat everything. He had grapes growing up against his building and the deer kept eating them and so finally I convinced him to put up electric fencing. But he was looking out his window one day and saw the deer touch the fence, and it knocked them back. He said, 'That really hurt them – I could see it –that was bad!' So that was the end of the electric fence."

Despite the deer, Bill did seem to enjoy gardening and plants in general. One fall when our chestnut tree was dropping a bounty of beautiful nuts in our yard, I filled a paper sack and took some to Bill, thinking he would enjoy roasting them as much as we did. He seemed pleased. But later, when I asked if he had eaten them yet, he told me he had potted them up, hoping for seedlings to plant.

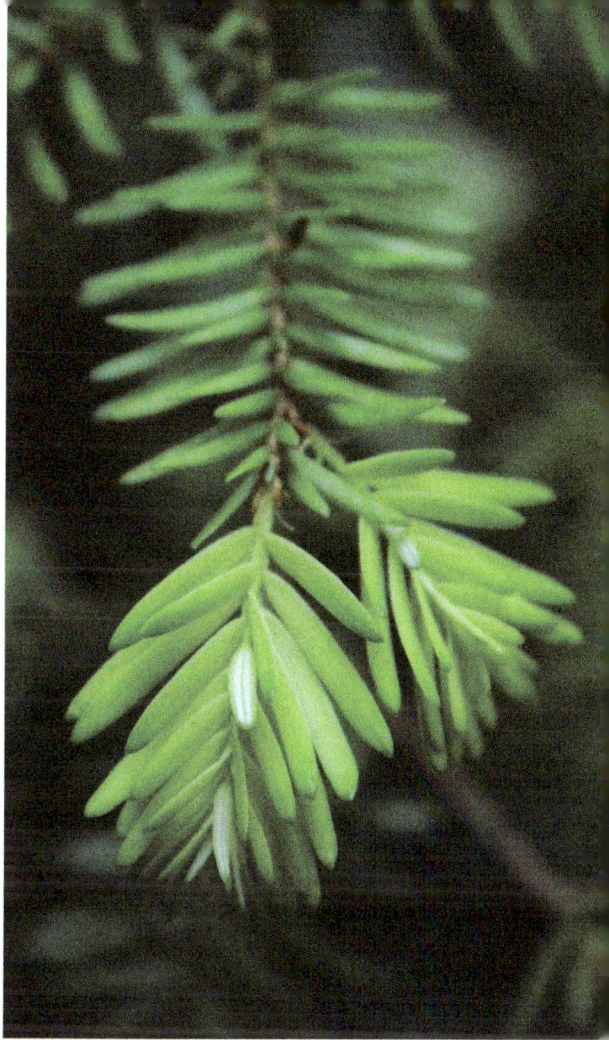

John Browne, an island musician and native plant expert, remembered a day Bill came to a Land Trust plant sale where he was selling. "I remember it was a particularly stormy day, and the pink blossoms from the trees in the parking lot were all over the ground. We had just gotten set up, getting plants out of the truck, when Bill and his friend Perry walked up. Perry says, 'Aw, you don't want any of this stuff.' But Bill picked up a skunk cabbage. 'I've wanted one of these for a while.' And Perry says, 'You could just dig one up somewhere.' And Bill says, 'No, I don't think that's the right thing to do.' So he bought the skunk cabbage and a *Rosa rugosa*."

John seemed to consider Bill a bit of a kindred spirit. "I enjoyed him because his mannerisms were of a particular school that I had become familiar with living down in coastal Oregon. There were these old fellows, some of them were widowers, some of them were bachelors, but they were essentially tool-handy, self-sufficient loners, didn't say much, didn't have a lot of friends, but they were really a wealth of information. I learned a lot from a number of these same kinds of guys as Bill. I could see farm implements and things around Bill's place that obviously had attracted him or that he'd had occasion to use at one time or another.

He had a soft spot for mechanical things and the value they could have, and just didn't want to see them wasted. It was obvious to me that was really important to him. Things having been a little different, I probably would have cultivated him more as a source of that kind of wisdom that is disappearing with guys of his generation."

ONE DAY I was driving my boys home from school, and right close to shore was a bald eagle sitting on a log and staring down into the water. We could see its huge yellow talons clutching the wood. It took a drink, dipping its curved beak into the water and tilting its head back. As we passed Bill's barn we saw him there, and stopped to tell him about the eagle. He said he often saw it sitting in that very spot. In the afternoon it liked to take a bath in the shallows, shaking water off its feathers "just like a robin in a birdbath."

Bill seemed to have a particular fondness for birds. Two expert birders with Vashon Audubon, Sue Trevathan and Carol Ferch, led

numerous field trips to Fisher Pond over the years. They met me in town to talk about their times with Bill.

"When we did birding classes with the school groups he was always so thoughtful," Carol said. "If there was a threat of rain, he'd put up a tent for us. He would tell the kids the story of how he got the property. He enjoyed watching the birds with us even though, truthfully, he wasn't very good at identifying birds or plants or animals."

Sue felt it was the big picture he cared more about, not any particular species. "He just enjoyed having a place where there were birds, and he couldn't care less what kind or how many there were," she said. "He liked the whole thing. It wasn't just one plant or bird that was special to him."

One early morning as I walked around the pond, I found Bill sitting with a group of clearly serious birders, their spotting scopes and binoculars all trained on the water. When I casually asked if they had seen anything special that morning, Bill smiled and gently chastised me. "They're all special," he said.

He liked taking care of the birds and other creatures in his own way, as he saw fit, not necessarily with formal ecological restoration goals in mind. For instance, Bill's friend Harry told me, every spring he would buy a thousand rainbow trout to stock the pond.

"They had big tankers full of 6 or 8 inch trout and they'd hose them out into his pond," Harry said. "He bought them to feed the ospreys and otters and eagles. He said they weren't for people to eat, and he wouldn't let me fish in there. He'd let children fish, but not me," he laughed. "We used to sit and watch the otters. First there'd be some little bubbles, then you'd see them come up with a big trout and crawl onto the log and eat it. Sometimes we'd see the eagles dive bomb the ospreys to steal their fish. That's why he bought all those trout. Just to feed the animals."

Bill was hospitable when conservation groups brought naturalists or foresters to assess his property, but he didn't necessarily follow their advice. Rayna Holtz is an island naturalist, reference librarian, and Audubon board member who taught ecology to elementary school classes. Her property is connected by trails to the north of Fisher Pond.

"Vashon Audubon leaders liked to stop and see the wide variety of wintering ducks, and summer broods of wood duck babies," she told me. "One summer, yellow pond lilies showed up for the first time in Bill's pond. They added color and interest, and it seemed like a nice addition at first. In just a few short years, however, they seemed to take over and eliminate much of the open water for diving birds. Audubon members decided to volunteer to help Bill clear some patches. I approached Bill when I saw him by the pond one afternoon and conveyed their offer. 'Why would I do that?' he asked, looking slightly amused at my earnestness. I explained how the lilies were clogging the water and their dying foliage created anaerobic conditions that were hard on water quality. 'I didn't plant those lilies,' he told me. 'Some duck must have brought them in. They just came. So I guess I'll let them be.'"

Just letting things be seemed to be Bill's general approach. He was genuinely curious to see what would happen in the pond if he didn't interfere too much. And he had a healthy, old-fashioned skepticism of experts.

Dave Warren, who was the executive director of the Land Trust at the time, told of visiting the pond with a Canadian forester who was promoting sustainable, low-impact management methods. He was leading a group along the main trail, assessing the forest, and Bill was walking along with them. The forester stopped at the base of one old fir, pointing out its flaws, how it leaned, its early signs of disease. "I'd probably take

that one out," he said, and moved on down the trail. Just then there was a shrill cry overhead, and a bald eagle that had been perched at the top of the tree took flight and soared out over the pond. Bill leaned over to Dave and said quietly, "I think I'll leave that one."

Bill had tried several times to reestablish the forest on the previously logged corner of 115th and Bank Road, but blackberries and scotch broom always took over before the trees could grow up. One winter, Dave Warren offered Bill some saplings from the annual Land Trust tree sale.

"Dave and I volunteered to plant them," Rayna remembered. "Bill met us there and we spent an afternoon hacking openings in the blackberries and digging holes for the tiny saplings. Dave and I were naïve to think those trees had any chance at all against the entrenched blackberries! I remember feeling a bit uncomfortable with Bill's amused skepticism.

He seemed pretty sure this was wasted effort, but he played along with us since we were so eager. I doubt a single one of those trees survived."

"It was terrible," Dave agreed. "Maybe three or four survived out of 300 cedars and 200 firs we planted. He'd already tried it before us. While we were all enthusiastic, Bill was saying, 'Yeah, yeah, we'll see.'"

Rayna's husband Jay Holtz, a retired landscape contractor, noted Bill's insights about such things. "Bill had a keen sense of human fallibility, and would often look aside with a wry smile while somebody was pontificating about something. He knew most of us didn't really know what we were talking about. And he also knew we have a tendency to make big proclamations about saving this or that. Meanwhile, he'd actually been protecting his land on his own for all those years."

EVEN THOUGH FISHER Pond was private property, more and more people began to visit over time, walking the trail that Bill maintained himself around the pond. In general, visitors were mindful of the privilege, but Bill was not shy about confronting someone if they were doing something he didn't approve of.

Rayna recalled a woman who would ride her horse through Bill's property, but she was pushy about it and finally Bill denied her access. She returned later with a homemade apple pie and tried to change his mind. "You know, I'd like to take your pie but I consider it a bribe, and I don't want you riding here." He refused the pie and sent her away.

Harry Bebow recalled a similar incident. "Some guy came riding a big horse down from the youth hostel and Bill got a bit angry. He saw what the horse's hooves were doing to all the plants along the trail and he said, 'I don't allow horses down here. It would damage the flowers.' So the guy asked which way he should go to get back home. Bill said to go out past the barn to Bank Road. The guy complained that was way too far. Bill said, 'Too bad!'

"When you walked down to the pond with him you had to be careful because he would not let you step on the plants. 'Pay attention and don't step in the middle,' he'd say, because of the flowers and little plants

growing there, even though some of them were weeds. He wouldn't even let you kill the slugs. It had to be just the way it was in nature."

John Browne, the native plant expert, once asked Bill how he felt about having people visiting his property. "As long as they behaved he didn't mind," John said. "But he wanted people to be careful on the trail, to pay attention to where they step. And he showed me some native evergreen violets, *Viola sempervirens,* a little flat yellow flower, and the only truly evergreen violet. There was a patch of them, and still is, I think,

but they're not common. He paid attention. Maybe he didn't know what they were, but he knew of them and paid attention and he didn't want people scuffing them and tramping on them and digging them up."

Shirley Ferris is a high school counselor and long-time islander who visited the pond for many years. "I respected Bill for never having a *No Trespassing* sign," she said. "He commanded respect somehow just by his humility and his presence. It was so interesting that people never really took advantage. You feel like it's sacred in a way when you go there. There's a very special spirit about that place. We went there for years without ever seeing him. I talked with him in later years when I felt more comfortable being there, knowing it was okay. He'd talk about his cats or making jam, all the native plants, and he was always interested in both my boys. He was a very sweet man. But he was shy, too, and I think people respected that. He was very unusual and wonderful in a way that you don't find very often."

FISHER POND IS never more popular than during the rare cold winters when it freezes over and people come to ice skate. Shirley had invited me to her high school office along with her long-time friend Linda Peterson. We sat around a table looking over Linda's photographs of people skating on the pond which were taken over several decades.

Linda and her husband Gary are known and loved for lugging boxes of ice skates down to the pond for anyone to borrow. "We'd gather up old skates from everybody – we had 60 or 70 pairs – and bring them to the pond when it froze, and just line the skates up. You could try them on and trade them around and see what worked. Each night we'd put them on our pool table and pull the liners out to dry. Sometimes we'd find a pair of ice skates left on our front porch. People would just drop them off, and expect us to add them to the collection."

In one photo, her son is six months old, bundled in a stroller on the ice. In the next, he is a tall young man on skates. Other pictures show informal hockey games with overturned buckets for goals. In one, there's a young girl with her arms spread wide, spinning on her skates in

the sunshine. In another, a boy is sitting on a crate doing homework by lantern light.

"Everybody has always been very sensible about when to go out and when not to," Linda said. "We'd come out with the drill to make sure there was at least two or three inches of ice. Those people who know ice, they called the shots. Neil here was one of them – he played hockey in

Boston and every time the pond froze he'd bring the sticks and organize the kids into teams.

"Here's the boy who fell in that year. There was an area roped off with buckets and orange tags, because it was thin there at the edges. But he was just at the age to push limits and he went through the ice. Just up to his waist, though. That's the fun thing about skating there – it isn't very deep. I can't remember who pulled him out. He was cold but he was fine."

Linda recalled a time when Bill was standing on shore watching the scene, and she realized he was the man who owned the pond. "We skated over and waved, and he came down onto the ice. We poured him some hot chocolate, and that's when he told us that he couldn't really invite people out to skate because of insurance reasons. But since we all just showed up there on our own, uninvited, he felt that was okay."

Linda's stories reminded me of one winter day when we were still new to the island. My family and I walked through snow from our house to the pond to find a gathering of people on the ice. We had never seen the pond frozen, and were charmed by the scene. Old and young and in-between, people were skating or just skidding along, some pushing strollers or pulling children in sleds. Some had brought their dogs. There was even a heater set up where kids were lacing up their skates by the road.

We walked gingerly out onto the ice with our boys, watching skaters spin and glide all around us. A man named Neil skated over to chat with my husband, and then offered to take my four-year-old Rowan for a spin. I didn't know the man or the ice, and pointed to a long crack where water was welling up and spilling onto the ice. "Oh, that's nothing to worry about," Neil assured me. Then he scooped my son up into his arms and sped away low and fast over the ice, over the crack, into the afternoon shadows, Rowan's gleeful laughter fading in the distance. A winter sun shone low through the trees, backlighting the circles and curves that countless blades had carved – a graceful tracery of intertwined paths, a record of the community's passages over the pond.

Humans aren't the only ones who enjoy the pond in winter. Naturalist Rayna Holtz told me about one very cold January morning she was out walking with her husband. "Jay and I walked through the frozen woods to Bill's pond, tiptoeing the last few hundred yards because we could hear odd noises. Peering through bushes near the picnic table, we saw two or three otters playing with the thin ice. We could hear muffled thumps as an otter swam underneath the ice, bumping it every few feet. Periodically it would erupt through in a fountain of water and tinkling pieces. One of the otters climbed onto a log, loped out to the end and somersaulted out and down, evidently relishing the sensation of shattering ice and splashing water. A few days later we returned, hoping to see them again, and ran into Bill there. He said they were regular guests. He thought it was likely that the otters worked their way from Fern Cove up Shinglemill Creek, rested at his pond, and then crossed into the Judd Creek drainage, following its tributaries down into Quartermaster Harbor."

THE TOPIC OF protecting the pond and forest came up nearly every time a birding group or nature class visited, Rayna told me. "'Who is going to take care of this after you go?' someone would ask. I remember one of Bill's responses. 'You don't have to worry about that,' he said. 'I plan to live forever.' And he was almost straight-faced, just the corners of his mouth turning up and his eyes twinkling."

He always intended on preserving the land," his neighbor Bill Dille told me. "That was his intention for years. He didn't know quite how it was going to be done, but he knew he wasn't going to divide it up, he knew he wasn't going to log it, and he wasn't going to let it go."

Rayna recalled that one of Bill's friends, a young woman who gardened with him one summer, came to see her at the library. "She explained to me that one of the things they were talking about was his land, that he wanted it to stay together and he was thinking of giving it to the water district. She thought they might put in a well and draw down the water, and the level of the pond could drop. She also tried to talk him out of donating it to the park district because she thought they might clear the corner lot and put in a ball field. So he was obviously discussing some of these things."

Rayna's husband Jay added, "Bill was casting around for some group that would be permanent. Initially, he didn't believe the Land Trust had any kind of track record, and he thought its people were all too young to be reliable. So he was considering other options. Dave Warren of the Land Trust wasn't the only one to talk to him about preserving his land, but Dave was the most persistent."

"He had his ups and downs," Dave told me. "He was very prickly sometimes. One time I went to Bill with a conservation easement, a legal document that goes with the land in perpetuity. They're typically 25 or 30 pages long. But I had stripped it down to a little over two pages, taken everything out that might be a little sticky for Bill. And I went over it with him real carefully, then left it with him and said if he had any problems to give me a call. When I got to the Land Trust the next day, Bill was there, and across the top of the document he'd written in red capital letters, NO WAY! And it was almost all red-lined.

"So I said that we should talk it over, but he didn't want to talk and was kind of walking away and I was trying to keep him engaged. And Bill said 'You're raising your voice. I don't want to listen to you anymore.' Which made me feel even worse. I said, 'I'm sorry, but I certainly want to continue to work with you.' And he said, 'Well, that may be, but I'm not interested in an easement on my land,' and he walked out. So for maybe four or five months we didn't have any contact."

Priscilla Beard was working on the Shinglemill watershed protection grant at that time. "I think what finally convinced him to donate his property was seeing the maps we had drawn up, because it was obvious how critical his property was to the entire watershed we were trying to protect. Dave had worked for years talking with him about different ways to protect his land. But Bill didn't think the Land Trust was going to be around very long. He said there was a lot of passion but no management. He just wanted to make sure we had some protection."

While Bill may have been uncertain about the Land Trust, he had limited options for preserving his land after he was gone. He had no wife or children, and his sisters weren't interested in the property except to sell it. He wanted the property to go directly to the community somehow without the IRS taking a piece of the profits. Eventually, he gave his land away through a complex arrangement in which the Park District would own Fisher Pond and the Land Trust would steward it going forward. When the $1.5 million Shinglemill grant was awarded, Bill donated his half of that money to a trust created for purchasing additional watershed properties and easements, and for ongoing management of the pond.

"It's worked out pretty well for me," Bill told one interviewer. "I'm warm and dry. I can walk in the woods and look at the pond and watch the birds. I plan on staying here until they bury me."

Dave Warren has vivid memories of the day Bill signed his land over to the Land Trust.

"I asked Bill if it was a go, and he said he was ready. So I brought him over to Patrick Cunningham's escrow office after hours. There were lots of aerial photos of the island from the 30s and 40s, and Bill walked around the room pointing things out. Patrick had grown up on the island about the same time Bill started coming over, so they knew some of the same people from that era, and that eased Bill's tension a little bit.

"And all the while there was the document on the table. And I remember seeing it there and thinking *is Bill really going to do this?* Because Bill had come close a couple times before, but then decided against it. Finally we all sat down. And there was the paper on the table between us as we continued to talk. Then Bill looked down and he read the whole thing through (he would always read very carefully to make sure what he was agreeing to) and finally he picked up the pen. And I was pretty nervous. I remember kind of rubbing my thumbs under the table.

"He bent over to sign the document, but then he stopped and looked up at the ceiling, and he said, 'May God help them.' And it had not hit me until that moment. You know, I thought this would be great for conservation, for trying to preserve the island, that this would be another important piece, a prize, an achievement. But then suddenly I felt this huge weight on my shoulders: how are we going to take care of it like Bill did? He loved this place, it was his home, and he had given his life to the pond. Who was I so presumptuous to think that we could carry on and give the land the kind of attention it needs? It really hit me then, the weight of the responsibility."

WHEN I LEARNED that Bill had donated his land, I started thinking about organizing a neighborhood potluck to thank him. I talked it over

with Priscilla and the idea soon grew into a bigger kind of gathering, an island event at the pond sponsored by the Land Trust that would become an annual celebration known as Bill Fisher Day.

So on a bright fall day in September 1998, Bill's quiet yard was transformed into a festive scene. There were tents streaming with crepe paper and balloons, tables draped in colorful cloths, dozens of homemade pies. Huge bouquets held autumn flowers and wild grasses. Folding chairs were set in the shade of apple trees. A crowd of friends and neighbors gathered for music and speeches and stories about Bill.

After the many expressions of appreciation and thanks, Emma Amiad from the Park District summed things up. "Today we celebrate a person of greatness. Bill Fisher is a humble man and shy person who has resisted fanfare as have many other benefactors. But his overwhelming generosity is just too great a thing not to celebrate here. To give a special place is to give your heart. Mr. Fisher has given his spirit to this community in this gift of the land that he loved so much. And for that he will be remembered for generations, for his love of place, and his willingness to share that which is most precious to him. It is hard to find words to express gratitude for such generosity. So as both a grateful citizen of Vashon Island and as president of the Vashon Park District Board, I'll keep it simple and say as others have before me: Thanks, Bill."

Then the engraved boulder, which had come from Priscilla's nearby property, was formally unveiled and presented to Bill. He smiled, shy and silent, with his hands in his pockets, looking at the rock. For a moment it seemed he might not say anything at all. But then he took the microphone and spoke. "I'm not really on the program, but I wanted to thank you all for coming. It's really kind of wonderful to see us all out here together. Well, I really don't have much to say. So, thank you again."

Later in the afternoon I noticed Bill in his upstairs window taking pictures and waving. He was alone up there, smiling, looking down on us all.

"When I first asked him if he'd let us do Bill Fisher Day, he was reluctant," Priscilla told me later. "But then he said, 'Let's walk around the pond and talk about this.' So we walked and I asked him what his

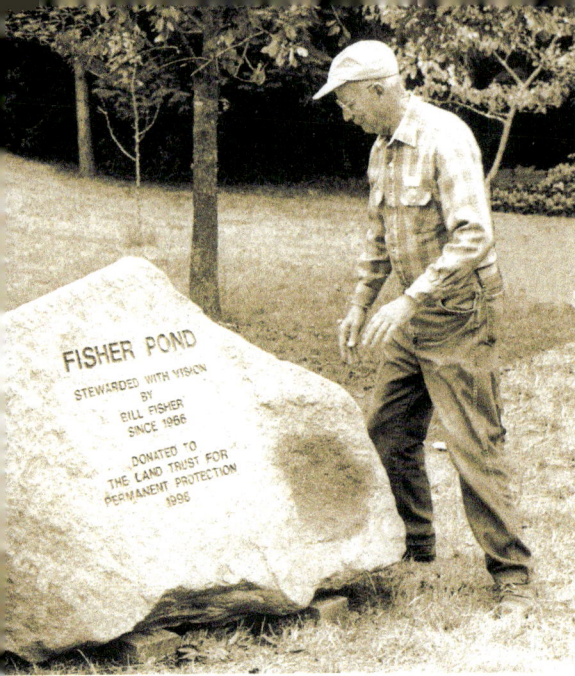

favorite food was and he said, 'Hands down, pie.' So I said, 'What about a celebration with just pie?' And he said, 'Well, that would be okay. I could bring the ice cream.' He always seemed confident at Bill Fisher Day, serving ice cream and greeting people that way. I think he found his community at the end of his life here. When he donated his land, I think that changed him and gave him a purpose, to educate people about the pond."

IN THE FALL of 2002, a few weeks before the 5th annual Bill Fisher Day, we were walking back up the trail with Bill. "You have chickens, don't you?" he asked me. Maybe he was thinking of the fresh eggs I'd brought him a few times, along with leeks, zucchini, raspberries, whatever we were harvesting from the garden. "I've got something for you to feed them," he said, and went on up the trail ahead of us. When the boys and I got to the barn a few minutes later, there outside the door were two large coffee cans filled with finely crushed eggshells, clean and carefully saved. He must have disappeared into his room, because I knocked and called at both doors to say thank you and goodbye, but he didn't answer or even wave from the window. I kept meaning to bring him some eggs in return, but days passed, then a week or two. That was the last time I saw Bill.

The message on my answering machine was from Priscilla, telling me that our friend Bill was gone. He had shot himself the night before. A neighbor was out early in the morning looking for his black lab who lived most of the time down at Bill's place. He found the dog there with Bill, who was lying on the grass just outside his door.

"It was a really big shock when they called and told me," Harry Bebow said, "because I'd just talked to him that night. We were going up to see the girls – his sister and my daughter who live in Kingston – but he said, 'We'd better hold off because I think I have the flu. Better not come down for a while because we don't want to take it up to the girls.' I said I'd come down and talk with him about it.

'No, you'd better stay there,' he said, 'because I've got a thousand things to do tonight.' He did it late that night, after I got through talking to him. No indication that he had that on his mind. He had everything laid out on the kitchen table for his sister, and little notes attached to everything, his billfold, checkbook, bank book for his savings account. Everything was laid out, orderly, on the table. Those are the thousand things he had to do that night."

My family and I walked to the pond that evening and read a prayer. We brought a towhee feather and a pear from the tree he loved and we

set them on the boulder at the edge of the pond. Often our footsteps flushed small flocks of ducks – buffleheads, mallards, wood ducks or wigeons – or a heron or kingfisher hunted from shore. That day there was only stillness, the silver water, mist rising from the willows. But for an occasional flutter or splash, there was no sound. Nothing moved.

While my family headed home, I walked around the barn to Bill's door where someone had scattered flower petals over the place he had lain on the ground. When I finally looked up, I saw he had left all his birdfeeders full.

A WEEK LATER, the fifth annual Bill Fisher Day became a memorial service where tears were shed and stories were told.

One of the most memorable to me was the briefest. "After I became Director of the Land Trust," Julie Burman told the crowd, "I decided to pay a visit to Bill Fisher to thank him for his generous gift of the pond and to ask him for any advice he might have for me in my new position. He asked me three questions: 'Can you drive a hard real estate bargain? Can you judge a man's character? Do you love the land?'"

Naturalist and poet Ann Spiers was one of the people who had worked with Bill Fisher as he moved to donate his land to the community. "As property steward for the Land Trust, I walked the land many times with Bill, he showing me the yellow violets, I showing him the rattlesnake plantian. If I walked away with a jar of his fruit preserves, I was well paid," she said. Ann put her feelings into a poem that spoke for many of us that day.

Here where we women fall in love with old men,

we stand in their gravel driveways,

taking home their blackberry jam,

slow conversations about the practical,

carving meaning into the last afternoons.

When we drive off, they think about us,

re-sort the small, medium and large ratchets,

take the rototiller out for a final turn,

feel pain flurry through their secret bodies,

they who had no children and no loves

to scent their sparky days and achy dawns.

Where are the old dogs they feed?

And now we women who fell in love

again phone around, gather poems and pies,

fluff the bouquets up front – dahlias,

vine maple, crab apple, sunflowers,

anything orangey, autumnly, homegrown –

and get the midday together

to come down the driveway once again,

and grind our teeth, saying how

we hate it when the good ones do that,

how they step outside in the moon night,

how one by one they leave us, how they die.

Ann Spiers

At the end of the service, I walked away from the crowd, left the tables laid with food and flowers, all the conversations. I entered the woods where there was no trail, just a tangle of roots and rotting logs, thickets of shrubs. Near the pond, I brushed past a huckleberry bush and saw the fawn lying beneath it. Its tiny bones were clean and white against the dark earth, intact, undisturbed, a perfect skeleton. It might have been sleeping, so graceful was its repose. I left it untouched. When I returned a week later, the bones had vanished.

Harry Bebow didn't attend the memorial service. "It took me about a month before I could realize he was gone," he said. "Even today, months later, I can't bring myself to go down to the pond. I just have to let it heal awhile first. Because we used to spend so much time sitting together down at that picnic table. I had immediate thoughts of what did I say or do? I've tried going over and over it, but then I realized it was his health that did it. He was talking to me once about his cancer operation, how painful it was. He had never been in a hospital before and he hated it. "Knowing him as well as I did, I know he must have been suffering. He knew I would've helped him, but he didn't want to be treated again, he didn't want to be a burden on anybody, and he didn't want to go through that again. He was a remarkable man and a very good friend. I miss him today."

Carolyn Buehl and her husband Evan live on acreage adjacent to the pond and were close friends of Bill for many years. Evan helped build the green barn, and did bulldozing projects around the property. "Nobody can keep someone else alive if they choose not to be here," Carolyn said to me. "But if you were good to that person, as best you can be, even though we're all human and fallible, then you need to be at peace with those feelings and your relationship. He loved us and we loved him. And I miss him.

He was a generous soul in many ways. But after Bill died, Evan said, 'I didn't really know the guy.' And Evan knew him better than almost anyone."

Sometime later an auction was arranged to clear the remainder of Bill's countless possessions from his apartment, workshop and yard. A crowd gathered by the old green barn, drawn by the auctioneer's call. The bidding had begun. We were there, neighbors and strangers, to look into rooms, to assess belongings, to assign value to what could be taken away. We had come to distribute the goods of a man's lifetime. Inside his workshop old tools lined the walls – calipers, hand-drills, pliers and planes – hung on pegs and outlined in pencil so each could be taken, then returned to its place. Among them all, one was missing. My eyes traced the empty periphery, a line that shaped what was gone, that defined, as I could not, the boundaries of an absence.

John Browne was there that day. "That auction was really something. I picked up a few hand-tools and bid on a couple of old coaster-brake, one-speed bicycles from the 50s he had taken really good care of. But man, the incredible number of things he had there, the lumber and arti-facts and tools and projects. I bought the guts of an old RCA Victrola. It looks like it's all there and it could be spinning 78s again sometime in the future if I can put it back together. "I still have an admiration for him for that. Some people rescue people, some people rescue cars, and he had a world of things there that he felt close to and had some emotions about, and that he thought needed to be taken care of. It's a side of him that was precious, and that energy continues to flow through the community."

"There's one more thing I remember," John said. "I asked Bill about harvesting some of the native crabapples on the edge of the pond. They're really tasty, sour as all get out, and when they turn translucent gold they sort of ferment inside the skin on the tree. I asked him if I could have some of them to make up some preserves, and he thought about it, didn't say anything for a while, and we talked about other stuff. And when I asked him again he said, 'Well, no, I don't think so. You probably could find them someplace else. The crows seem to be pretty fond of them, so I'd just as soon leave what I can for the birds.' Pretty thoughtful. He was a hell of a steward. He did care about the place, and it wasn't a sense of ownership. It was a sense of stewardship. There really is a difference. He took it all pretty seriously. He wanted to leave it better than he found it. And he did."

SOMETIME AFTER THE auction, the Land Trust gave me two cardboard boxes full of Bill's photographs and personal documents. One afternoon I spread everything across my kitchen table, half hoping to find something unexpected, a new insight into Bill's life, perhaps some missing piece. But the photos were simply of the things he cared about. The pond in all seasons. His picnic table. Skunk cabbage, willow, salmonberry, salal. Otters swimming, deer at rest. His cat on a tractor, a black dog sleeping in the grass. Family photos, ferry rides, friends at yard sales. One picture caught my eye, a yellow flower filling the frame that looked at first like a zinnia or dahlia. But then I realized what I was seeing – a dandelion flower set in a glass and carefully photographed. A weed appreciated without prejudice, its ordinariness ignored in favor of its beauty. That one photograph I kept for myself. The rest I put away. I closed my notebook and left the cluttered house. I walked to the road and turned toward Fisher Pond, where I would look for wild violets, and admire the weeds, and pay attention to where I step.

FISHER POND

STEWARDED WITH VISION
BY
BILL FISHER
SINCE 1966

DONATED TO
THE LAND TRUST FOR
PERMANENT PROTECTION
1998

Bill Fisher with Laurie and her sons, Rowan and Ian, 1998.

LAURIE STEWART has worked as an environmental paralegal and science writer, and is currently manager at the Vashon Bookshop. She has lived on Vashon Island since 1994 with her husband, two sons, and several generations of sheep, chickens, cats and dogs.

CPSIA information can be obtained
at www.ICGtesting.com
Printed in the USA
FSOW04n1805270717
36652FS